I0794148

Our Wonderful World of... Buildings

By Rebecca Phillips-Bartlett

KidHaven Publishing

Published in 2024 by
KidHaven Publishing, an Imprint of Greenhaven Publishing, LLC
2544 Clinton St., Buffalo, NY 14224

Written by: Rebecca Phillips-Bartlett
Edited by: Elise Carraway
Designed by: Amelia Harris

Photo Credits
Images are courtesy of Shutterstock.com—with thanks to Getty Images, Thinkstock Photo, and iStockphoto.
Recurring images – Naticka, Olga1818. Cover – cosmaa, Magnia, happpy.designer, mentalmind, danceyourlife, Macrovector, Slowga, Seita, PrintablesPlazza, Save nature and wildlife, CryptoSkylark, T. Lesia, charnsitr. 2 – Sean Hsu, Vector Tradition. 3 – Slowga. 4–5 – Djent, noir_illustration. 6 – Wangkun Jia, Robert Crum. 7 – Sean Pavone, Eduard Moldoveanu, ivector. 8 – Jon Chica. 8–9 – Vector Tradition. 9 – Fotos593. 10 – Kanuman, Nikiforov Alexander. 11 – Viacheslav Lopatin, NotionPic. 12 – Wesley Lazarus, LineTale. 13 – Pranesh Luckan. 14 – Kirill Neiezhmakov. 15 – Ivan Kurmyshov, Naeblys. 16 – AlexAnton, VectoRaith. 17 – Vi design, saiko3p, NotionPic. 18 – Sean Hsu. 18–19 – Dernkadel. 19 – Luciano Mortula - LGM, Daniela Constantinescu. 20 – Andrew H McFarlane. 20–21 – Slowga. 21 – myphotobank.com.au. 22 – happpy.designer, Vector Tradition, ivector. 23 – Slowga, Naeblys, aurielaki, NotionPic.

Cataloging-in-Publication Data
Names: Phillips-Bartlett, Rebecca, 1999-.
Title: Buildings / Rebecca Phillips-Bartlett.
Description: Buffalo, New York: KidHaven Publishing, 2024. |
Series: Our wonderful world of… | Includes glossary and index.
Identifiers: ISBN 9781534546172 (pbk.) | ISBN 9781534546189 (library bound) | ISBN 9781534546196 (ebook)
Subjects: LCSH: Building--Juvenile literature. | Engineering--Juvenile literature. | Structural engineering--Juvenile literature.
Classification: LCC TA634.P487 2024 | DDC 624.1--dc23

Manufactured in the United States of America

CPSIA compliance information: Batch #CW24KH: For further information contact Greenhaven Publishing LLC at 1-844-317-7404.

Please visit our website, www.greenhavenpublishing.com.
For a free color catalog of all our high-quality books, call toll free 1-844-317-7404 or fax 1-844-317-7405.

Find us on

CONTENTS

Words that look like this can be found in the glossary on page 24.

WELCOME TO OUR WONDERFUL WORLD!

Our wonderful world is full of brilliant buildings. Every country is different and unique. One thing that sets each country apart is the different buildings they have.

We are going on a <u>tour</u> around the world! In each country, we will meet a guide. They will tell us about some of the brilliant buildings in their country.

DID YOU KNOW?

The different floors in a building are also known as stories.

THE UNITED STATES

The New York Public Library

The New York Public Library has millions of books, magazines, and other items. The main reading room is as long as a soccer field. The library is guarded by two stone lions.

The Empire State Building

The Empire State Building is a skyscraper in New York City. Skyscrapers are very tall buildings. New York has many skyscrapers. The Empire State Building is often lit up with colorful lights.

DID YOU KNOW?

The lights change color for important events and holidays.

COLOMBIA

Hi, I am Juan. I live in Colombia.

Las Lajas Sanctuary

Las Lajas Sanctuary is a church in Colombia. The church was built on the side of a cliff over the Guáitara River. Some people believe that many miracles have happened there.

Zipaquirá Salt Cathedral

The Salt Cathedral of Zipaquirá used to be a salt mine. Now, it is an underground church. The people who worked in the mine dug very deep. The church is around 656 feet (200 m) underground.

DID YOU KNOW?

Even the statues are made of salt.

ITALY

Hello, I am Riccardo. I live in Italy.

The Leaning Tower of Pisa

The Leaning Tower of Pisa is a bell tower in Pisa. The tower was not meant to lean, but now that is what it is known for!

The Colosseum

The Colosseum is almost 2,000 years old. It is the largest amphitheater in the world. An amphitheater is a large outdoor theater. People used to visit the Colosseum to watch sporting events such as gladiator fights.

SOUTH AFRICA

15 Alice Lane Towers

The 15 Alice Lane Towers were once known as the Dancing Towers. The towers have an unusual curvy shape. They are covered in a pattern made of glass, concrete, and metal.

FNB Stadium

FNB Stadium is the largest stadium in Africa. The stadium is also known as the Calabash. Its round shape is based on a type of fruit called a calabash, which can be used as a cooking pot.

THE UNITED ARAB EMIRATES

Hello.
My name is
Saeed. I live
in the U.A.E.

Burj Khalifa

The Burj Khalifa is the world's tallest building. It is more than 2,625 feet (800 m) tall! The top of the tower is so high up that it sometimes sways in the wind.

Dubai Mall

Next to the Burj Khalifa is one of the world's largest shopping malls. The Dubai Mall has more than 1,000 shops. It even has a large ice-skating rink inside.

INDIA

Taj Mahal

The Taj Mahal is known as one of the world's most beautiful buildings. It was built to hold the tomb of an emperor's wife. Her name was Mumtaz Mahal. The building is named after her.

Meenakshi Temple

One of the oldest temples in India is Meenakshi Temple. It is a Hindu temple in the south of India. The temple contains around 30,000 colorful statues.

JAPAN

Hello! I am Reina. I live in Japan.

Sensō-ji

Sensō-ji is the oldest Buddhist temple in Japan's capital city, Tokyo. Next to the temple there is a tower called a pagoda.

Osaka Castle

Osaka Castle is one of the most famous buildings in Japan. The castle is decorated with golden tigers and other animals from Japanese folktales.

DID YOU KNOW?

This is a Shachi. It has the head of a tiger and the body of a fish.

AUSTRALIA

Flinders Street Station

Flinders Street Station is the oldest train station in Australia. It was built in Melbourne in 1854. It's still a working station today and a popular place for visitors!

Sydney Opera House

Sydney Opera House is a theater. It is one of Australia's most famous buildings. Sydney Opera House was only meant to take 4 years to build, but it actually took 14 years!

DID YOU KNOW?

Sydney Opera House is meant to look like a ship's sails.

A WORLD OF BRILLIANT BUILDINGS

On our tour, we have seen many brilliant buildings. From temples to train stations, each was built for a different reason. Many of them are an important part of their country's history.

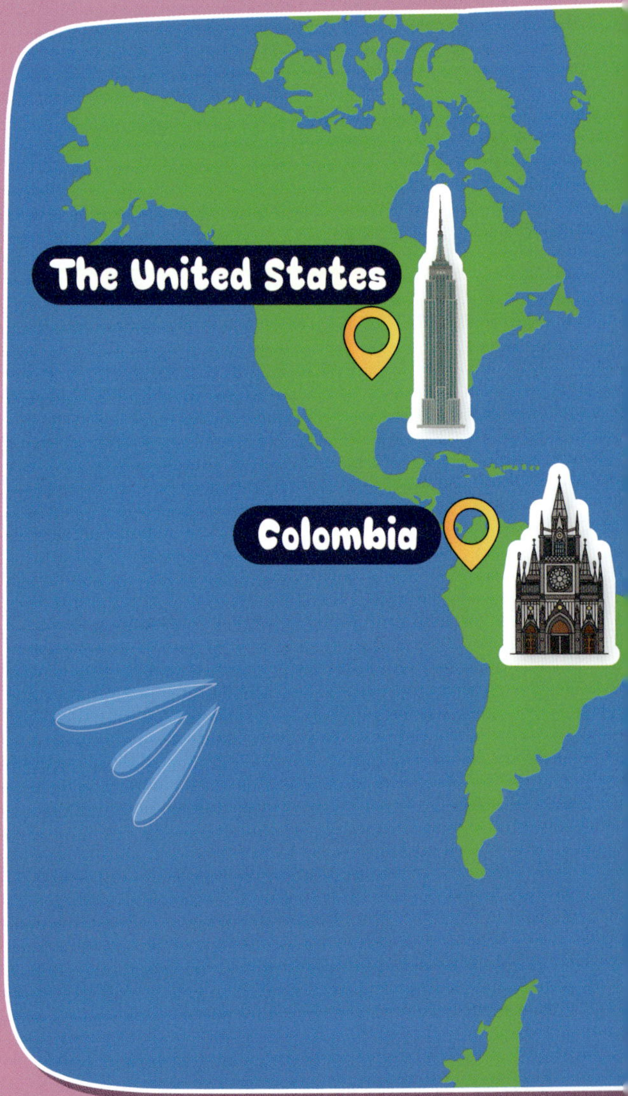

There are brilliant buildings in every country. Imagine you are a tour guide. If someone came to your country, what buildings would you show them?

GLOSSARY

church a Christian place of worship

emperor a ruler of a large area of land called an empire

folktales stories passed down within families and countries

gladiator a person who fought for entertainment in ancient Rome

mine a pit that people have made to take valuable things out of the ground

miracles amazing events that cannot be explained and are often thought to have happened supernaturally

temples places of worship

tomb a place people are buried after they die

tour a trip that involves visiting many different places

unique unlike anything or anyone else

INDEX